The Periodic Table

Halogens, Noble Gases and Lanthanides and Actinides

Children's Chemistry Book

Speedy Publishing LLC
40 E. Main St. #1156
Newark, DE 19711
www.speedypublishing.com

In this book, we're going to briefly cover the Periodic Table of Elements. Then, we're going to take an in-depth look at the Halogens, Noble Gases, and Lanthanides and Actinides, which are groups of elements within the periodic table.

WHAT IS THE PERIODIC TABLE OF ELEMENTS?

The periodic table is a way of organizing all the elements on our planet that scientists have discovered. The number of protons that each element has in its nucleus, which is its atomic number, determines how the elements are organized in rows. Each of the horizontal rows is called a period. The table has either seven or eight periods depending on how you interpret them.

Periodic Table

OF ELEMENTS

1	2	3	4	5	6	7	8	9	10	11	12	13	14	15	16	17	18
1.008 1 H Hydrogen																	[illegible] 2 He Helium
6.941 3 Li Lithium	9.012 4 Be Beryllium											10.811 5 B Boron	12.011 6 C Carbon	14.007 7 N Nitrogen	15.999 8 O Oxygen	18.998 9 F Fluorine	20.180 10 Ne Neon
22.990 11 Na Sodium	24.305 12 Mg Magnesium											26.982 13 Al Aluminum	28.086 14 Si Silicon	30.974 15 P Phosphorus	32.066 16 S Sulfur	35.453 17 Cl Chlorine	39.948 18 Ar Argon
39.098 19 K Potassium	40.078 20 Ca Calcium	44.956 21 Sc Scandium	47.867 22 Ti Titanium	50.942 23 V Vanadium	51.996 24 Cr Chromium	54.938 25 Mn Manganese	55.845 26 Fe Iron	58.933 27 Co Cobalt	58.693 28 Ni Nickel	63.546 29 Cu Copper	65.38 30 Zn Zinc	69.723 31 Ga Gallium	72.631 32 Ge Germanium	74.922 33 As Arsenic	78.971 34 Se Selenium	79.904 35 Br Hydrogen	84.798 36 Kr Hydrogen
84.468 37 Rb Rubidium	87.62 38 Sr Stronium	88.906 39 Y Yttrium	91.224 40 Zr Zirconium	92.906 41 Nb Niobium	95.95 42 Mo Molybdenum	98.907 43 Tc Technetium	101.07 44 Ru Ruthenium	102.906 45 Rh Rhodium	106.42 46 Pd Palladium	107.868 47 Ag Silver	112.411 48 Cd Cadmium	114.818 49 n Indium	118.711 50 Sn Tin	121.760 51 Sb Antimony	127.6 52 Te Tellurium	126.904 53 I Iodine	131.294 54 Xe Xenon
132.905 55 Cs Cesium	137.328 56 Ba Barium	57-71	178.49 72 Hf Hafnium	180.948 73 Ta Tantalum	183.84 74 W Tungsten	186.207 75 Re Rhenium	190.23 76 Os Osmium	192.217 77 Ir Iridium	195.085 78 Pt Platinum	196.967 79 Au Gold	200.592 80 Hg Mercury	204.383 81 Ti Thallium	207.2 82 Pb [illegible]	208.980 83 Bi Bismuth	[208.982] 84 Po Polonium	209.987 85 At Astatine	222.018 86 Rn Radon
223.020 87 Fr Francium	226.025 88 Ra Radium	89-103	[illegible] 104 Rf Rutherfordium	[262] 105 Db Dubnium	[266] 106 Sg Seaborgium	[264] 107 Bh Bohrium	[269] 108 Hs Hassium	[illegible] 109 Mt Meitnerium	[illegible] 110 Ds Darmstadtium	[272] 111 Rg Roentgenium	[277] 112 Cn Copernicium	Unknown 113 Uut Ununtrium	[289] 114 Fl Flerovium	Unknown 115 Uup Ununpentium	[298] 116 Lv Livermorium	Unknown 117 Uus Ununseptium	Unknown 118 Uuo Ununoctium

Series															
Lanthanide Series	138.905 57 La Lanthanum	140.116 58 Ce Cerium	140.908 59 Pr Praseodymium	144.243 60 Nd Neodymium	144.913 61 Pm Promethium	150.36 62 Sm Samarium	151.964 63 Eu Europium	157.25 64 Gd Gadolinium	158.925 65 Tb Terbium	162.500 66 Dy Dysprosium	164.930 67 Ho Holmium	167.259 68 Er Erbium	168.934 69 Tm Thalium	173.055 70 Yb Ytterbium	174.967 71 Lu Lutetium
Actinide Series	227.028 89 Ac Actinium	232.038 90 Th Thorium	231.036 91 Pa Protactinium	238.029 92 U Uranium	237.048 93 Np Neptunium	244.064 94 Pu Plutonium	243.061 95 Am Americium	247.070 96 Cm Curium	247.070 97 Bk Berkelium	251.080 98 Cf Californium	[254] 99 Es Einsteinium	257.095 100 Fm Fermium	258.1 101 Md Mendelevium	259.101 102 No Nobelium	[262] 103 Lr Lawrencium

Periodic Table of Elements

Li : Solid
Br : Liquid
O : Gas
Sg : Unknown

METALS

Alkali Metals · Alkaline Earth Metals · Lanthanoids · Actinoids · Transition Metals · Poor Metals

NONMETALS

Other Nonmetals · Noble Gases

	1	2	3	4	5	6	7	8	9	10	11	12	13	14	15	16	17	18
A	1 H Hydrogen 1.00794																	2 He Helium 4.002603
B	3 Li Lithium 6.941	4 Be Beryllium 9.012182											5 B Boron 10.811	6 C Carbon 12.0107	7 N Nitrogen 14.0067	8 O Oxygen 15.9994	9 F Fluorine 18.9984032	10 Ne Neon 20.1797
C	11 NA Sodium 22.98976928	12 Mg Magnesium 24.3050											13 Al Aluminium 26.9815386	14 Si Silicon 28.0855	15 P Phosphorus 30.973762	16 S Sulfur 32.065	17 Cl Chlorine 35.453	18 Ar Argon 39.948
D	19 K Potassium 39.0983	20 Ca Calcium 40.078	21 Sc Scandium 44.955912	22 Ti Titanium 47.867	23 V Vanadium 50.9415	24 Cr Chromium 51.9961	25 Mn Manganese 54.938045	26 Fe Iron 55.845	27 Co Cobalt 58.933195	28 Ni Nickel 58.6934	29 Cu Copper 63.546	30 Zn Zinc 65.38	31 Ga Gallium 69.723	32 Ge Germanium 72.64	33 As Arsenic 74.92160	34 Se Selenium 78.96	35 Br Bromine 79.904	36 Kr Krypton 83.798
E	37 Rb Rubidium 85.4678	38 Sr Strontium 87.62	39 Y Yttrium 88.90585	40 Zr Zirconium 91.224	41 Nb Niobium 92.90638	42 Mo Molybdenum 95.96	43 Tc Technetium (97.9072)	44 Ru Ruthenium 101.07	45 Rh Rhodium 102.90550	46 Pd Palladium 106.42	47 Ag Silver 107.8682	48 Cd Cadmium 112.411	49 In Indium 114.818	50 Sn Tin 118.710	51 Sb Antimony 121.760	52 Te Tellurium 127.60	53 I Iodine 126.90447	54 Xe Xenon 131.293
F	55 Cs Caesium 132.9054519	56 Ba Barium 137.327	57-71	72 Hf Hafnium 178.49	73 Ta Tantalum 180.94788	74 W Tungsten 183.84	75 Re Rhenium 186.207	76 Os Osmium 190.23	77 Ir Iridium 192.217	78 Pt Platinum 195.084	79 Au Gold 196.966569	80 Hg Mercury 200.59	81 Tl Thallium 204.3833	82 Pb Lead 207.2	83 Bi Bismuth 208.98040	84 Po Polonium (208.9824)	85 At Astatine (209.9871)	86 Rn Radon (222.0176)
G	87 Fr Francium (223)	88 Ra Radium (226)	89-103	104 Rf Rutherfor- dium (261)	105 Db Dubnium (262)	106 Sg Seaborgium (266)	107 Bh Bohrium (264)	108 Hs Hassium (277)	109 Mt Meitnerium (268)	110 Ds Darmstadtium (271)	111 Rg Roentgenium (272)	112 Uub Ununtrium (285)	113 Uut Ununtrium (284)	114 Uuq Ununquadium (289)	115 Uup Ununpentium (288)	116 Uuh Ununhexium (292)	117 Uus Ununseptium	118 Uuo Ununoctium (294)

57 La Lanthanum 138.90547	58 Ce Cerium 140.116	59 Pr Praseodymium 140.90765	60 Nd Neodymium 144.242	61 Pm Promethium (145)	62 Sm Samarium 150.36	63 Eu Europium 151.25	64 Gd Gadolinium 157.25	65 Tb Terbium 158.92535	66 Dy Dysprosium 162.500	67 Ho Holmium 164.93032	68 Er Erbium 167.259	69 Tm Thulium 168.93421	70 Yb Ytterbium 173.054	71 Lu Lutetium 174.9668
89 Ac Actinium (227)	90 Th Thorium 232.03806	91 Pa Protactinium 231.03588	92 U Uranium 238.02891	93 Np Neptunium (237)	94 Pu Plutonium (244)	95 Am Americum (243)	96 Cm Curium (247)	97 Bk Berkelium (247)	98 Cf Californium (251)	99 Es Einsteinium (252)	100 Fm Fermium (257)	101 Md Mendelevium (258)	102 No Nobelium (259)	103 Lr Lawrencium (262)

The elements of hydrogen and helium make up the first short period of just 2 elements while the sixth period has 32 elements. As you move across a period or row and travel from left to right, the element at the leftmost edge of the table has only 1 electron in its outer shell, while the element at the rightmost edge has a full shell of electrons.

WHY ARE THE COLUMNS IN THE PERIODIC TABLE IMPORTANT?

Just like the rows in the table are important, the columns are important as well.

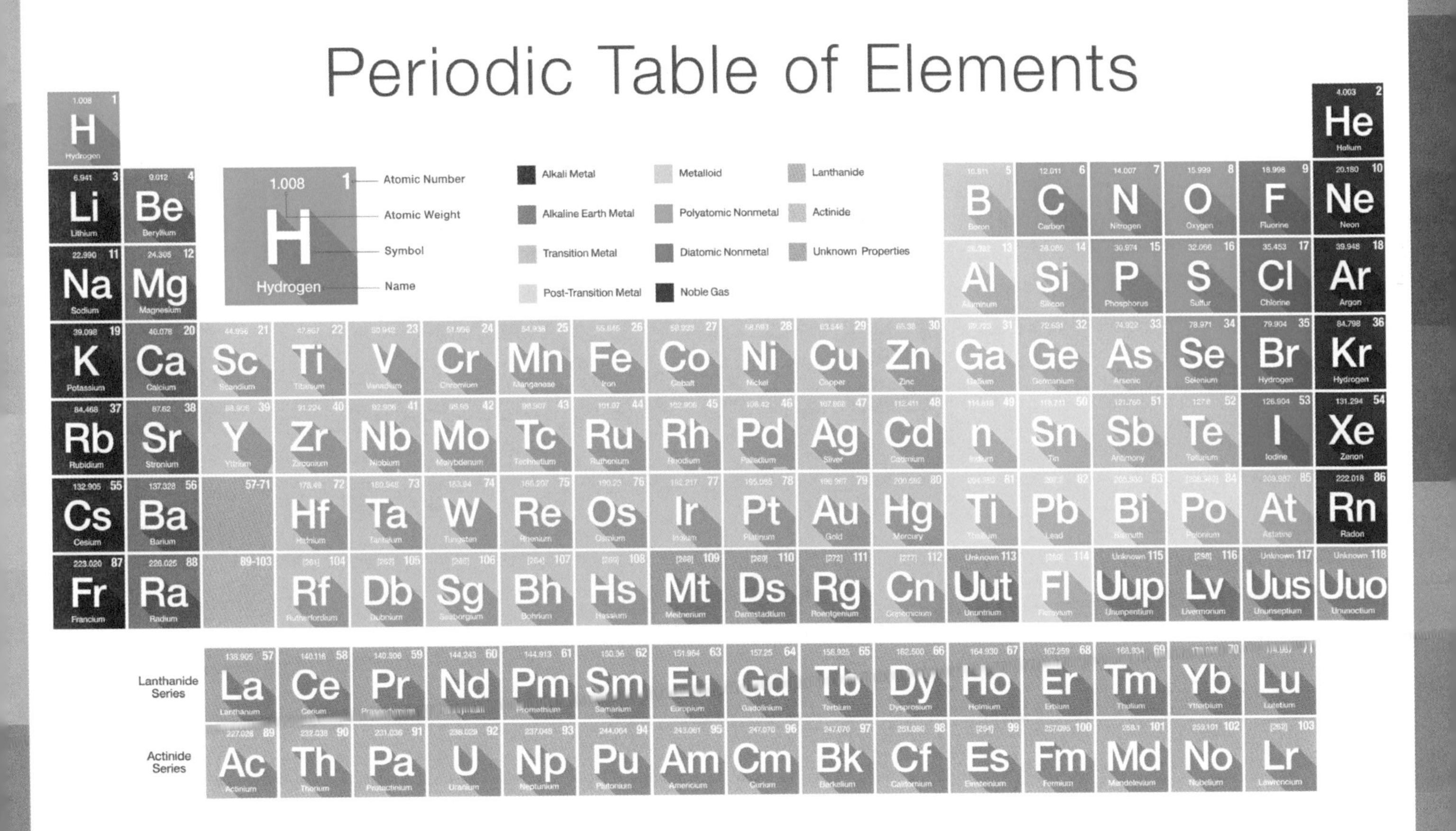
Periodic Table of Elements
1.008
1
H
Hydrogen
Atomic Number
Atomic Weight
Symbol
Name
Alkali Metal
Alkaline Earth Metal
Transition Metal
Post-Transition Metal
Metalloid
Polyatomic Nonmetal
Diatomic Nonmetal
Noble Gas
Lanthanide
Actinide
Unknown Properties
1 H Hydrogen
2 He Helium
3 Li Lithium
4 Be Beryllium
5 B Boron
6 C Carbon
7 N Nitrogen
8 O Oxygen
9 F Fluorine
10 Ne Neon
11 Na Sodium
12 Mg Magnesium
13 Al Aluminum
14 Si Silicon
15 P Phosphorus
16 S Sulfur
17 Cl Chlorine
18 Ar Argon
19 K Potassium
20 Ca Calcium
21 Sc Scandium
22 Ti Titanium
23 V Vanadium
24 Cr Chromium
25 Mn Manganese
26 Fe Iron
27 Co Cobalt
28 Ni Nickel
29 Cu Copper
30 Zn Zinc
31 Ga Gallium
32 Ge Germanium
33 As Arsenic
34 Se Selenium
35 Br Hydrogen
36 Kr Hydrogen
37 Rb Rubidium
38 Sr Stronium
39 Y Yttrium
40 Zr Zirconium
41 Nb Niobium
42 Mo Molybdenum
43 Tc Technetium
44 Ru Ruthenium
45 Rh Rhodium
46 Pd Palladium
47 Ag Silver
48 Cd Cadmium
49 n
50 Sn Tin
51 Sb Antimony
52 Te Tellurium
53 I Iodine
54 Xe Zanon
55 Cs Cesium
56 Ba Barium
57-71
72 Hf Hafnium
73 Ta Tantalum
74 W Tungsten
75 Re Rhenium
76 Os Osmium
77 Ir Iridium
78 Pt Platinum
79 Au Gold
80 Hg Mercury
81 Tl Thallium
82 Pb Lead
83 Bi Bismuth
84 Po Polonium
85 At Astatine
86 Rn Radon
87 Fr Francium
88 Ra Radium
89-103
104 Rf Rutherfordium
105 Db Dubnium
106 Sg Seaborgium
107 Bh Bohrium
108 Hs Hassium
109 Mt Meitnerium
110 Ds Darmstadtium
111 Rg Roentgenium
112 Cn Copernicium
Unknown 113 Uut Ununtrium
114 Fl Flerovium
Unknown 115 Uup Ununpentium
116 Lv Livermorium
Unknown 117 Uus Ununseptium
Unknown 118 Uuo Ununoctium
Lanthanide Series
57 La Lanthanum
58 Ce Cerium
59 Pr
60 Nd
61 Pm Promethium
62 Sm Samarium
63 Eu Europium
64 Gd Gadolinium
65 Tb Terbium
66 Dy Dysprosium
67 Ho Holmium
68 Er Erbium
69 Tm Thulium
70 Yb Ytterbium
71 Lu Lutetium
Actinide Series
89 Ac Actinium
90 Th Thorium
91 Pa Protactinium
92 U Uranium
93 Np Neptunium
94 Pu Plutonium
95 Am Americium
96 Cm Curium
97 Bk Berkelium
98 Cf Californium
99 Es Einsteinium
100 Fm Fermium
101 Md Mendelevium
102 No Nobelium
103 Lr Lawrencium

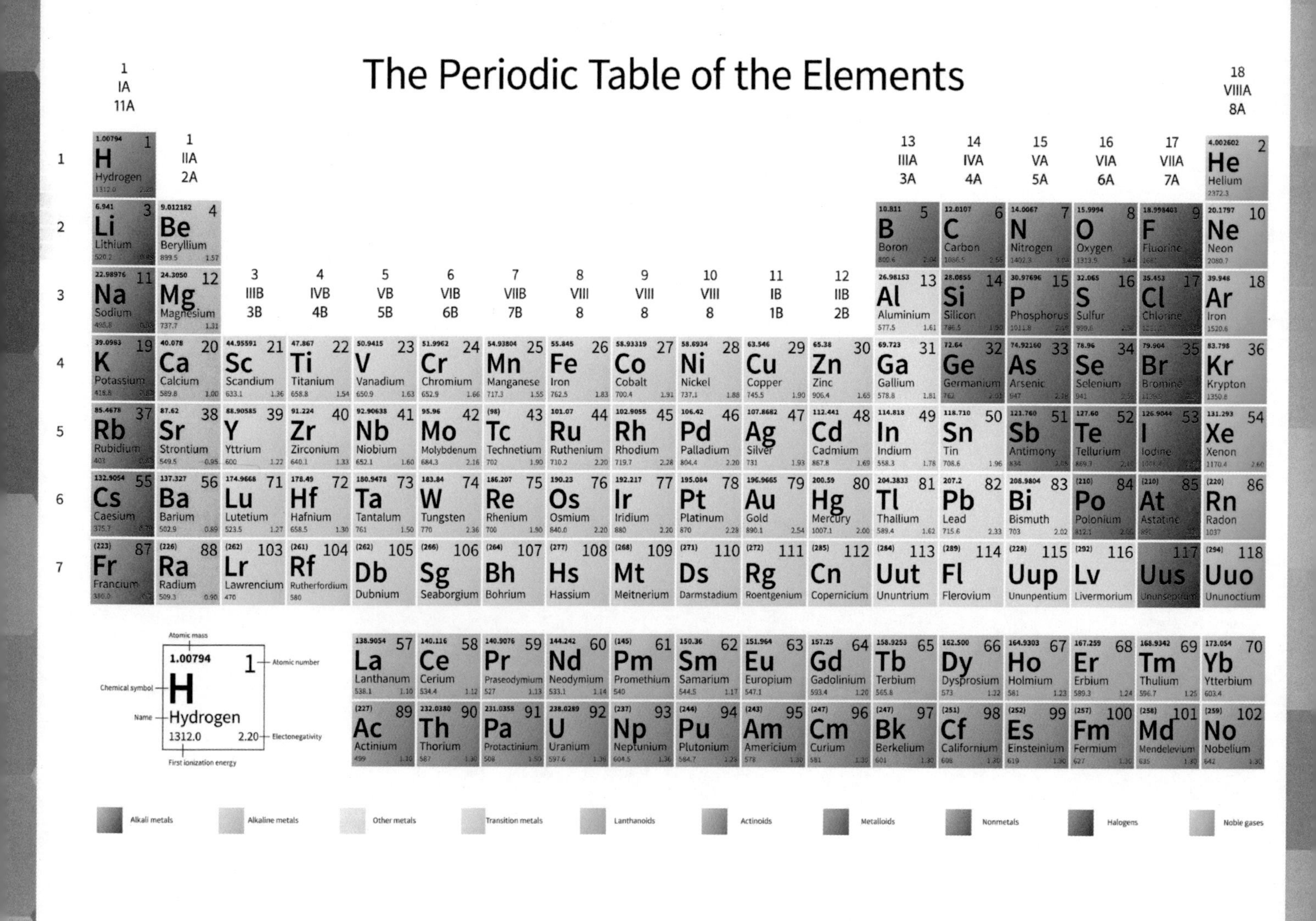

The Periodic Table of the Elements
1 IA 11A
1 IIA 2A
3 IIIB 3B
4 IVB 4B
5 VB 5B
6 VIB 6B
7 VIIB 7B
8 VIII 8
9 VIII 8
10 VIII 8
11 IB 1B
12 IIB 2B
13 IIIA 3A
14 IVA 4A
15 VA 5A
16 VIA 6A
17 VIIA 7A
18 VIIIA 8A
1
2
3
4
5
6
7
1.00794 1 H Hydrogen
4.002602 2 He Helium
6.941 3 Li Lithium
9.012182 4 Be Beryllium
10.811 5 B Boron
12.0107 6 C Carbon
14.0067 7 N Nitrogen
15.9994 8 O Oxygen
18.998403 9 F Fluorine
20.1797 10 Ne Neon
22.98976 11 Na Sodium
24.3050 12 Mg Magnesium
26.98153 13 Al Aluminium
28.0855 14 Si Silicon
30.97696 15 P Phosphorus
32.065 16 S Sulfur
35.453 17 Cl Chlorine
39.948 18 Ar Iron
39.0983 19 K Potassium
40.078 20 Ca Calcium
44.95591 21 Sc Scandium
47.867 22 Ti Titanium
50.9415 23 V Vanadium
51.9962 24 Cr Chromium
54.93804 25 Mn Manganese
55.845 26 Fe Iron
58.93319 27 Co Cobalt
58.6934 28 Ni Nickel
63.546 29 Cu Copper
65.38 30 Zn Zinc
69.723 31 Ga Gallium
72.64 32 Ge Germanium
74.92160 33 As Arsenic
78.96 34 Se Selenium
79.904 35 Br Bromine
83.798 36 Kr Krypton
85.4678 37 Rb Rubidium
87.62 38 Sr Strontium
88.90585 39 Y Yttrium
91.224 40 Zr Zirconium
92.90638 41 Nb Niobium
95.96 42 Mo Molybdenum
(98) 43 Tc Technetium
101.07 44 Ru Ruthenium
102.9055 45 Rh Rhodium
106.42 46 Pd Palladium
107.8682 47 Ag Silver
112.411 48 Cd Cadmium
114.818 49 In Indium
118.710 50 Sn Tin
121.760 51 Sb Antimony
127.60 52 Te Tellurium
126.9044 53 I Iodine
131.293 54 Xe Xenon
132.9054 55 Cs Caesium
137.327 56 Ba Barium
174.9668 71 Lu Lutetium
178.49 72 Hf Hafnium
180.9478 73 Ta Tantalum
183.84 74 W Tungsten
186.207 75 Re Rhenium
190.23 76 Os Osmium
192.217 77 Ir Iridium
195.084 78 Pt Platinum
196.9665 79 Au Gold
200.59 80 Hg Mercury
204.3833 81 Tl Thallium
207.2 82 Pb Lead
208.9804 83 Bi Bismuth
(210) 84 Po Polonium
(210) 85 At Astatine
(220) 86 Rn Radon
(223) 87 Fr Francium
(226) 88 Ra Radium
(262) 103 Lr Lawrencium
(261) 104 Rf Rutherfordium
(262) 105 Db Dubnium
(266) 106 Sg Seaborgium
(264) 107 Bh Bohrium
(277) 108 Hs Hassium
(268) 109 Mt Meitnerium
(271) 110 Ds Darmstadium
(272) 111 Rg Roentgenium
(285) 112 Cn Copernicium
(284) 113 Uut Ununtrium
(289) 114 Fl Flerovium
(228) 115 Uup Ununpentium
(292) 116 Lv Livermorium
117 Uus Ununseptium
(294) 118 Uuo Ununoctium
138.9054 57 La Lanthanum
140.116 58 Ce Cerium
140.9076 59 Pr Praseodymium
144.242 60 Nd Neodymium
(145) 61 Pm Promethium
150.36 62 Sm Samarium
151.964 63 Eu Europium
157.25 64 Gd Gadolinium
158.9253 65 Tb Terbium
162.500 66 Dy Dysprosium
164.9303 67 Ho Holmium
167.259 68 Er Erbium
168.9342 69 Tm Thulium
173.054 70 Yb Ytterbium
(227) 89 Ac Actinium
232.0380 90 Th Thorium
231.0358 91 Pa Protactinium
238.0289 92 U Uranium
(237) 93 Np Neptunium
(244) 94 Pu Plutonium
(243) 95 Am Americium
(247) 96 Cm Curium
(247) 97 Bk Berkelium
(251) 98 Cf Californium
(252) 99 Es Einsteinium
(257) 100 Fm Fermium
(258) 101 Md Mendelevium
(259) 102 No Nobelium
Atomic mass
1.00794 1 H Hydrogen 1312.0 2.20
Atomic number
Chemical symbol
Name
Electonegativity
First ionization energy
Alkali metals
Alkaline metals
Other metals
Transition metals
Lanthanoids
Actinoids
Metalloids
Nonmetals
Halogens
Noble gases

There are 18 groups within the table and each group has its own set of properties. By studying the way the groups are organized, chemists can make predictions about the behavior and chemical properties of certain elements.

ABBREVIATIONS IN THE PERIODIC TABLE

The periodic table contains abbreviations for all the names of the elements. Sometimes these abbreviations are easy to figure out and sometimes they're not.

PERIODIC TABLE OF THE ELEMENTS

Long Shadow Style

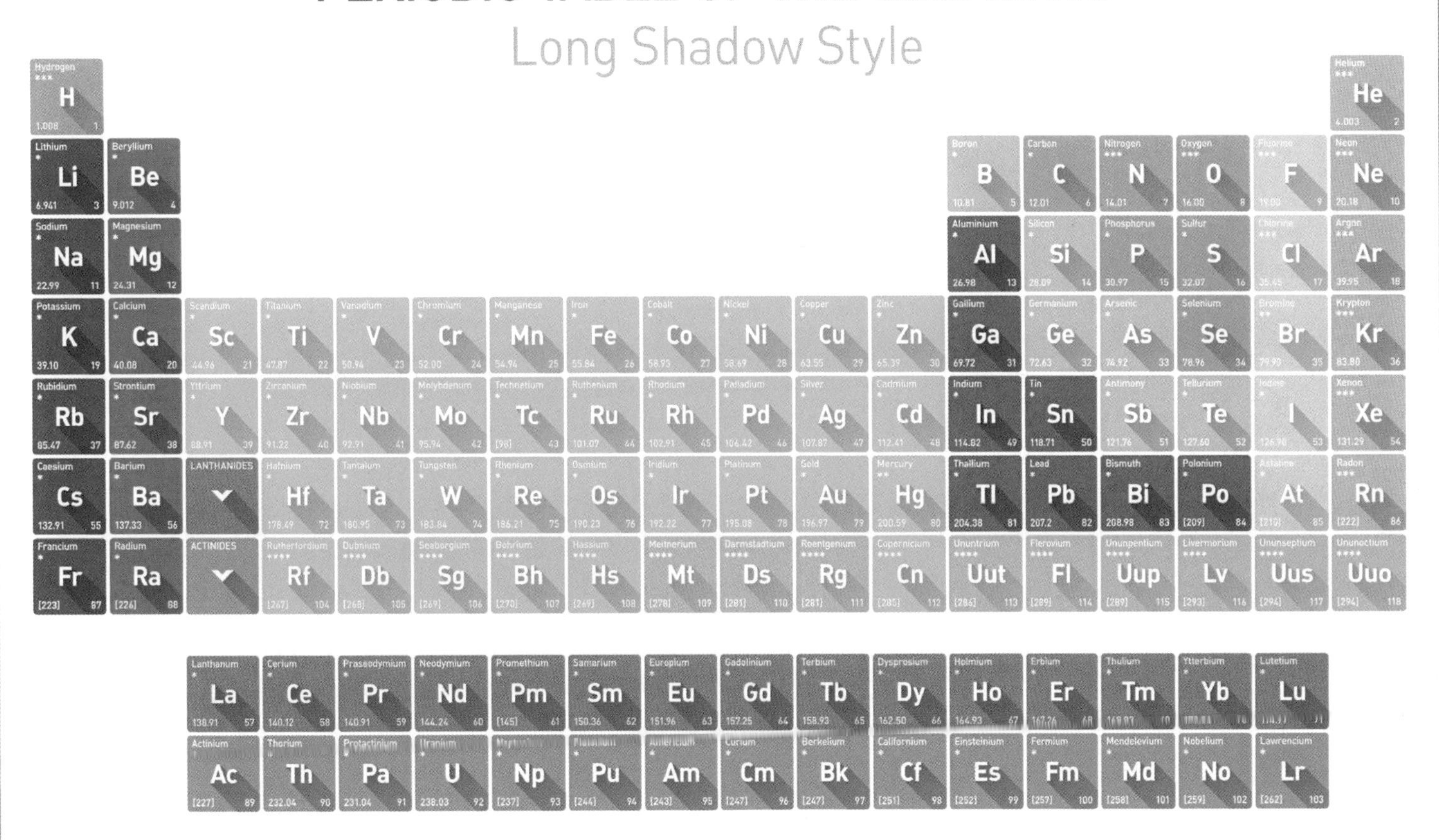

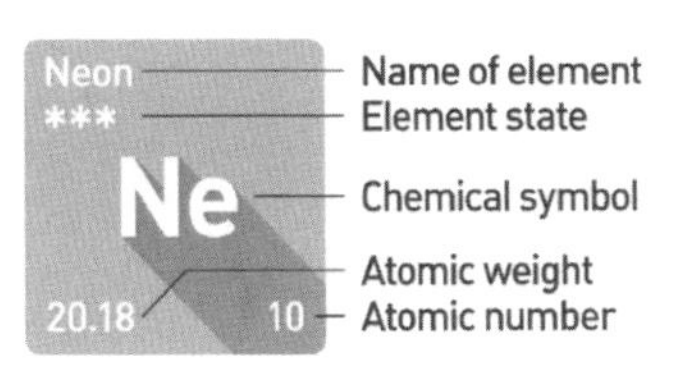

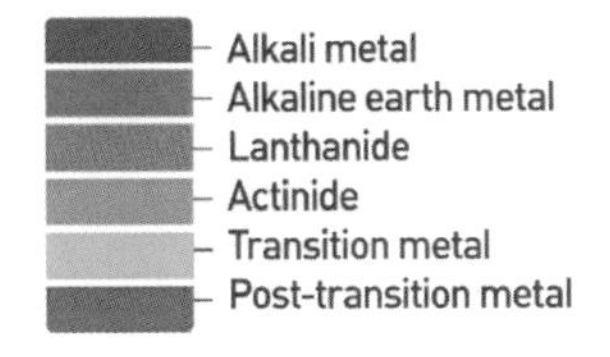

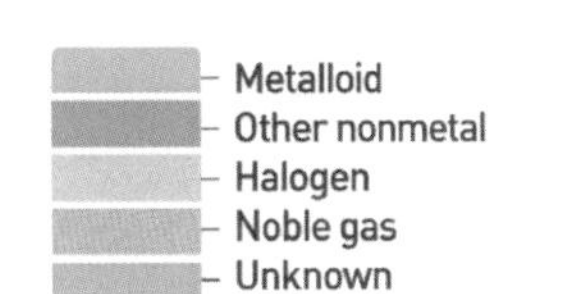

* Solid
** Liquid
*** Gas
**** Unknown

For example, the abbreviation HE stands for helium, but the abbreviation AU stands for gold. The abbreviation for gold comes from the Latin word for gold, which is aurum. Every letter in the alphabet except for J is used in the periodic table.

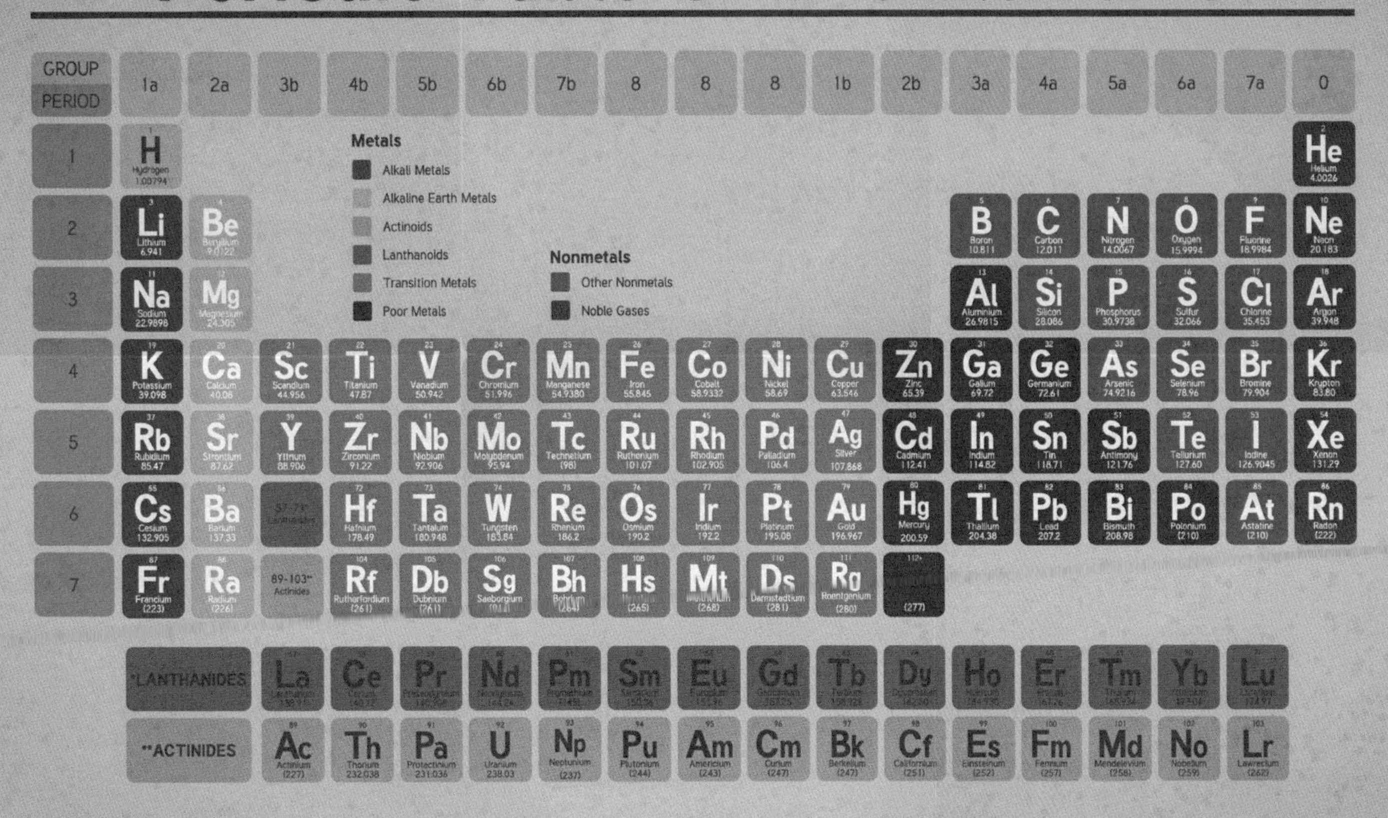

★★ Periodic Table Of The Elements ★★
GROUP
PERIOD
1a 2a 3b 4b 5b 6b 7b 8 8 8 1b 2b 3a 4a 5a 6a 7a 0
1 2 3 4 5 6 7
Metals
Alkali Metals
Alkaline Earth Metals
Actinoids
Lanthanoids
Transition Metals
Poor Metals
Nonmetals
Other Nonmetals
Noble Gases
H Hydrogen 1.00794
He Helium 4.0026
Li Lithium 6.941
Be Beryllium 9.01122
B Boron 10.811
C Carbon 12.011
N Nitrogen 14.0067
O Oxygen 15.9994
F Fluorine 18.9984
Ne Neon 20.183
Na Sodium 22.9898
Mg Magnesium 24.305
Al Aluminium 26.9815
Si Silicon 28.086
P Phosphorus 30.9738
S Sulfur 32.066
Cl Chlorine 35.453
Ar Argon 39.948
K Potassium 39.098
Ca Calcium 40.08
Sc Scandium 44.956
Ti Titanium 47.87
V Vanadium 50.942
Cr Chromium 51.996
Mn Manganese 54.9380
Fe Iron 55.845
Co Cobalt 58.9332
Ni Nickel 58.69
Cu Copper 63.546
Zn Zinc 65.39
Ga Gallium 69.72
Ge Germanium 72.61
As Arsenic 74.9216
Se Selenium 78.96
Br Bromine 79.904
Kr Krypton 83.80
Rb Rubidium 85.47
Sr Strontium 87.62
Y Yttrium 88.906
Zr Zirconium 91.22
Nb Niobium 92.906
Mo Molybdenum 95.94
Tc Technetium (98)
Ru Ruthenium 101.07
Rh Rhodium 102.905
Pd Palladium 106.4
Ag Silver 107.868
Cd Cadmium 112.41
In Indium 114.82
Sn Tin 118.71
Sb Antimony 121.76
Te Tellurium 127.60
I Iodine 126.9045
Xe Xenon 131.29
Cs Cesium 132.905
Ba Barium 137.33
Hf Hafnium 178.49
Ta Tantalum 180.948
W Tungsten 183.84
Re Rhenium 186.2
Os Osmium 190.2
Ir Iridium 192.2
Pt Platinum 195.08
Au Gold 196.967
Hg Mercury 200.59
Tl Thallium 204.38
Pb Lead 207.2
Bi Bismuth 208.98
Po Polonium (210)
At Astatine (210)
Rn Radon (222)
Fr Francium (223)
Ra Radium (226)
89-103** Actinides
Rf Rutherfordium (261)
Db Dubnium (261)
Sg Seaborgium
Bh Bohrium (264)
Hs (265)
Mt (268)
Ds Darmstadtium (281)
Rg Roentgenium (280)
(277)
*LANTHANIDES
La Ce Pr Nd Pm Sm Eu Gd Tb Dy Ho Er Tm Yb Lu
**ACTINIDES
Ac Actinium (227)
Th Thorium 232.038
Pa Protactinium 231.036
U Uranium 238.03
Np Neptunium (237)
Pu Plutonium (244)
Am Americium (243)
Cm Curium (247)
Bk Berkelium (247)
Cf Californium (251)
Es Einsteinium (252)
Fm Fermium (257)
Md Mendelevium (258)
No Nobelium (259)
Lr Lawrencium (262)

fluorine

F

9

chlorine

Cl

17

bromine

Br

35

iodine

I

53

astatine

At

85

WHAT ARE HALOGENS?

In the second column from the right side of the periodic table, in column 17, are elements in a group called the halogens. They are positioned to the left of the noble gases and right of the group called “other nonmetals.” There are five elements in this group and their names all end in “ine.” They are astatine, bromine, chlorine, fluorine, and iodine.

WHAT PROPERTIES MAKE HALOGENS SIMILAR?

In their outer shells, all of the halogens have seven valence electrons. They are just one electron short of having full shells and this means they are very reactive.

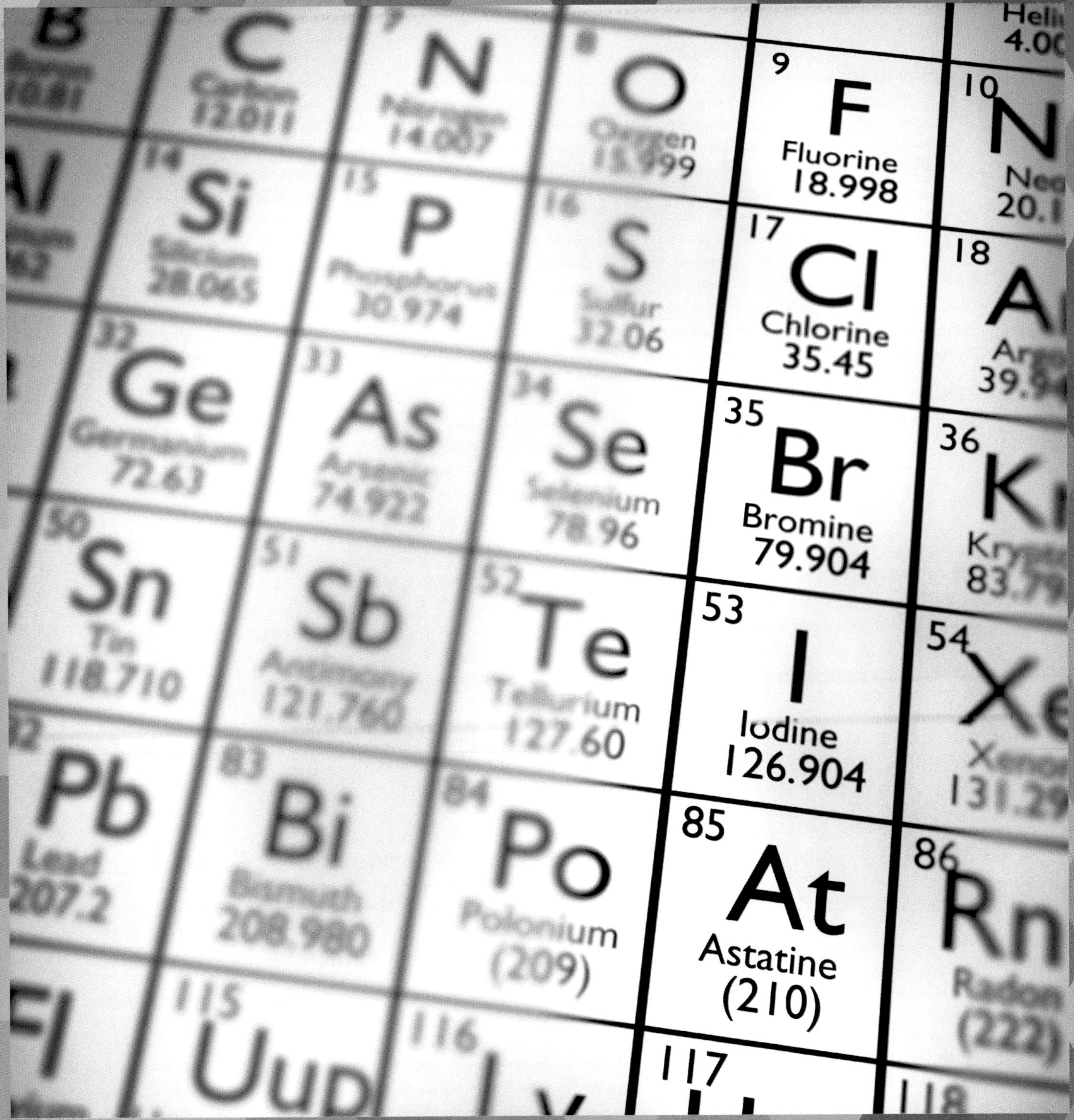

9
F
Fluorine
18.998

17
Cl
Chlorine
35.45

35
Br
Bromine
79.904

53
I
Iodine
126.904

85
At
Astatine
(210)

17

35.453

Cl

Chlorine

Reactive just means that they frequently bond with other elements. Fluorine is the most reactive of the halogen elements and it combines readily with most of the elements.

As you move down a column in the table, the elements get less and less reactive. The chemical properties of an element are slightly different than the properties of the element that appears above it in the table. Another similarity these elements have is that they all create acids when they are joined with hydrogen.

35

bromum

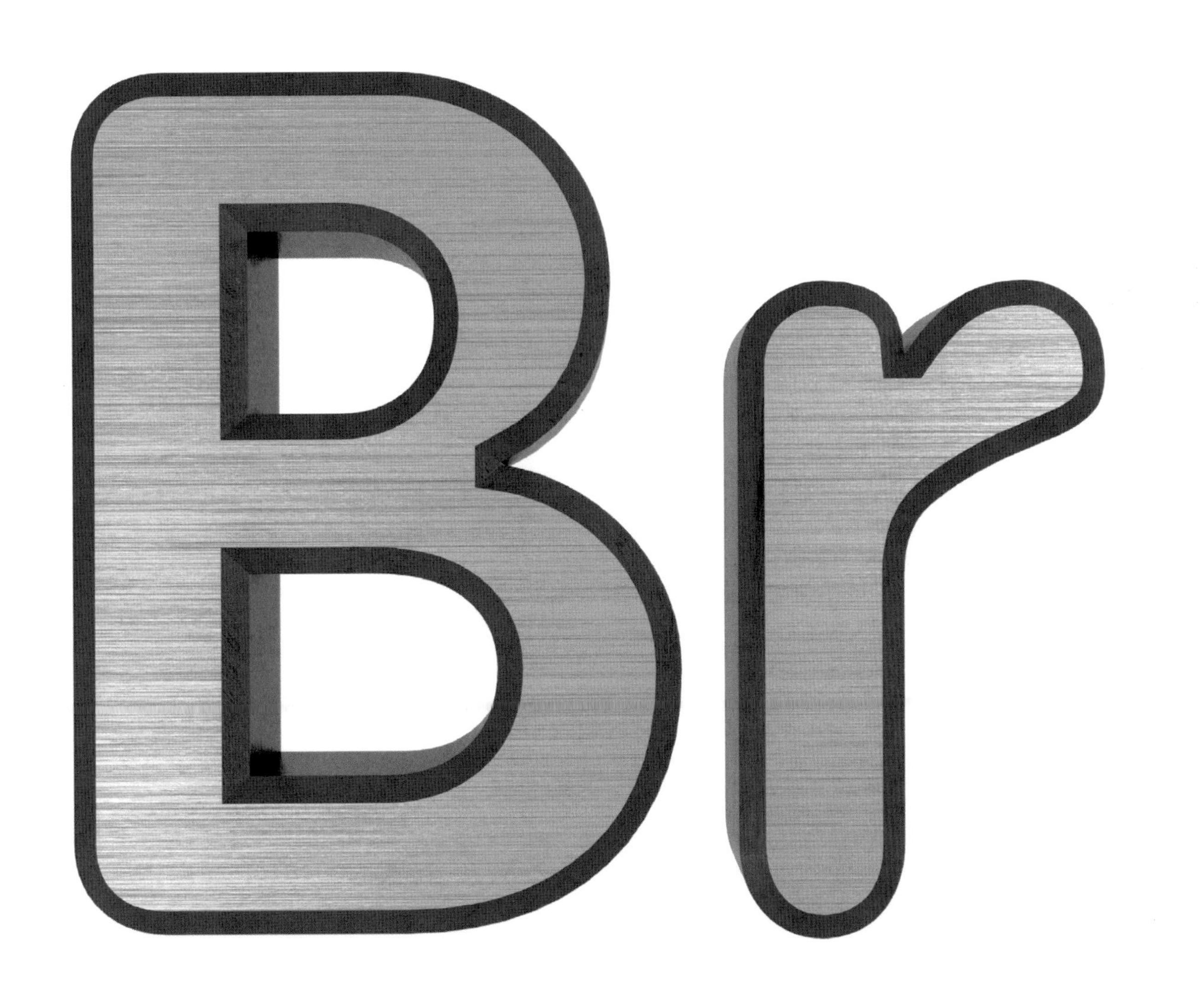

$4s^2 4p^5$

79,904

OF ELEMENTS
18
VIIIA
ATOMIC NUMBER
SYMBOL
NAME
15
VA
0
Fluorine
18.998
-2
+4
+6
17
Cl
Chlorine
35.453
-1
+1
+3
+5
+7
18
STATE
GAS
-4
+2
+4
C
Si
Ge
72.64
74.92
+2
+4
Sn
Tin
51
Sb
Antimony
121.76
127.6
131.29
35
-1
+1
83
Bi
+3
+5
84
Po
+2
+4
85
At
86
Rn
0
Pb

The word "halogen" comes from the Greek words that mean "to make salt." All five halogens easily form salt compounds. In fact, many of the salts in seawater are compounds that consist of a halogen combined with a metal element. An example of this is the compound magnesium chloride. The table salt that we use everyday in our food is sodium chloride, another such compound.

Another common characteristic of the halogens is that they have a strong odor. The element of bromine gets its name from the Greek word for “stench.”

9

fluorum

$2s^2 2p^5$

18,9984

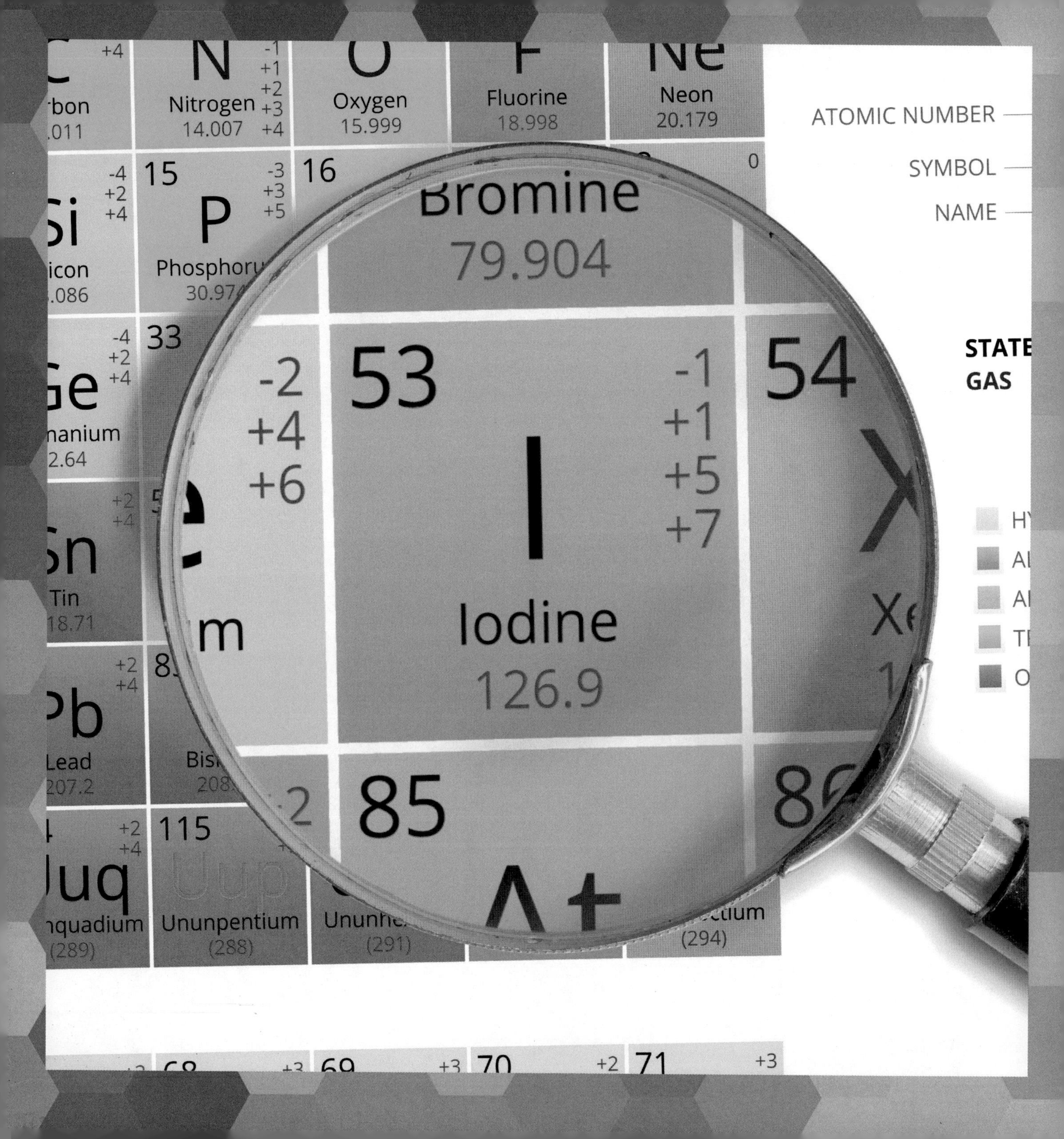

N
Nitrogen
14.007
-1
+1
+2
+3
+4
Oxygen
15.999
Fluorine
18.998
Neon
20.179
ATOMIC NUMBER
SYMBOL
NAME
15
P
Phosphorus
-3
+3
+5
16
Bromine
79.904
0
-4
+2
+4
33
STATE
GAS
53
I
Iodine
126.9
-1
+1
+5
+7
-2
+4
+6
54
Sn
Tin
Pb
Lead
207.2
85
115
Ununpentium
(288)
(291)
(294)
(289)
68
69
70
71

All the halogen elements have diatomic molecules, which simply means that in their natural form their molecules are made up of two atoms.

THE FORM OF HALOGENS IN STANDARD CONDITIONS

The halogen elements, under regular conditions, show up as all three of the types of matter. The elements of fluorine and chlorine are gases, the element of iodine and the element of astatine are solids, and then there's bromine, which is a liquid. The only element other than bromine that is a liquid in its natural state at around 70 degrees Fahrenheit is the element of mercury.

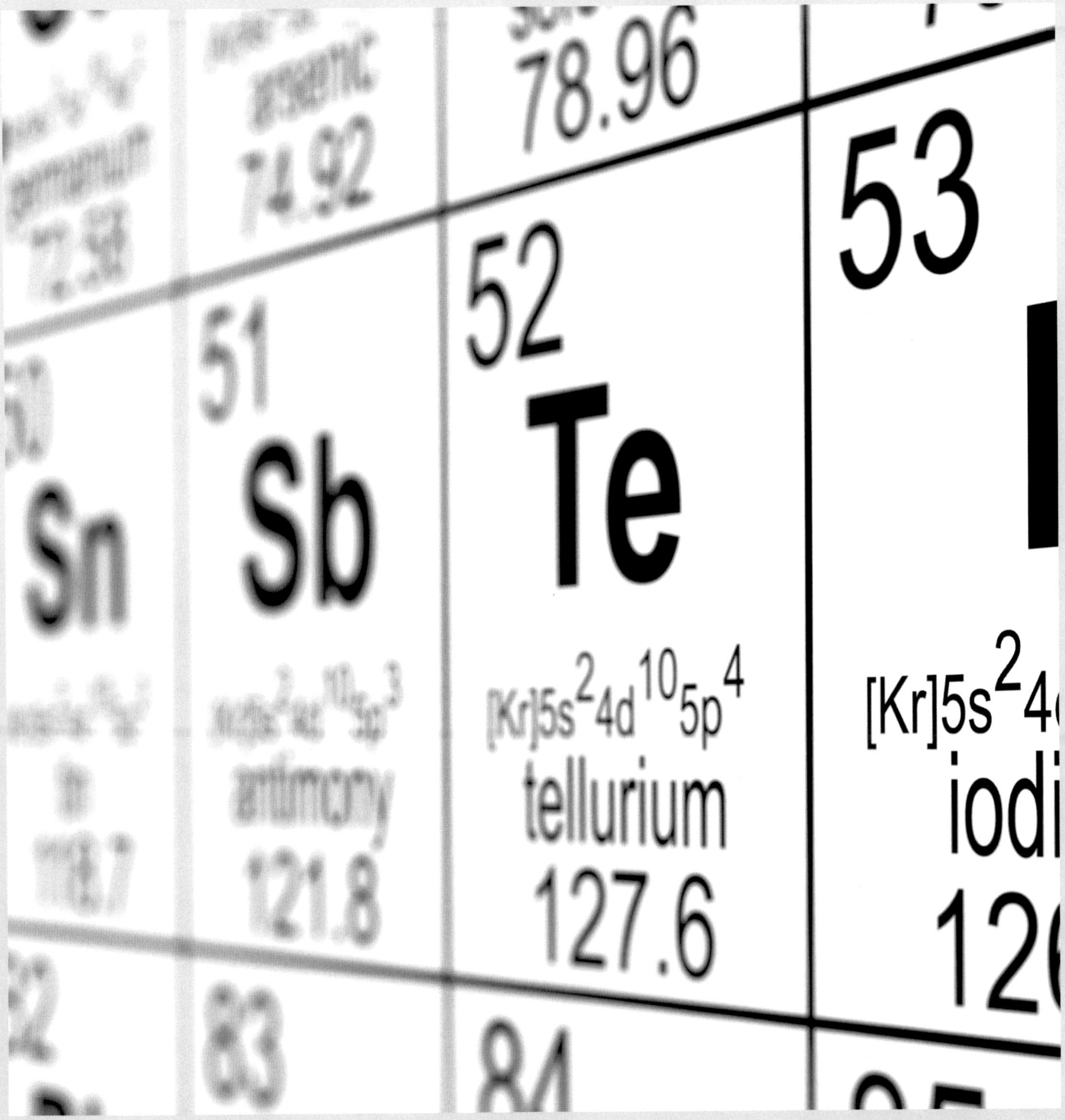

78.96

74.92

53

52

51

Sn

Sb

Te

[Kr]$5s^2 4d^{10} 5p^4$

tellurium

127.6

antimony

121.8

83

84

FLUORINE

The Earth's crust contains all five halogens with fluorine being the most abundant and astatine being the most rare.

FASCINATING FACTS ABOUT HALOGENS AND HALIDES

- Halogen light bulbs contain iodine and bromine. They give off brighter light than regular electric light bulbs. They're frequently used to flood stadiums with light at nighttime.
- Fluorine is so deadly that taking in air that contains 0.1% of it causes death.
- Salts made with chlorine are used for swimming pool water to kill germs.
- When a halogen reacts with and combines with another element, the simple compound that is formed is called a halide. A common example that you know about is table salt, which is sodium chloride. Another that you may have heard of, is fluoride, which is often added to drinking water to help us prevent tooth decay.

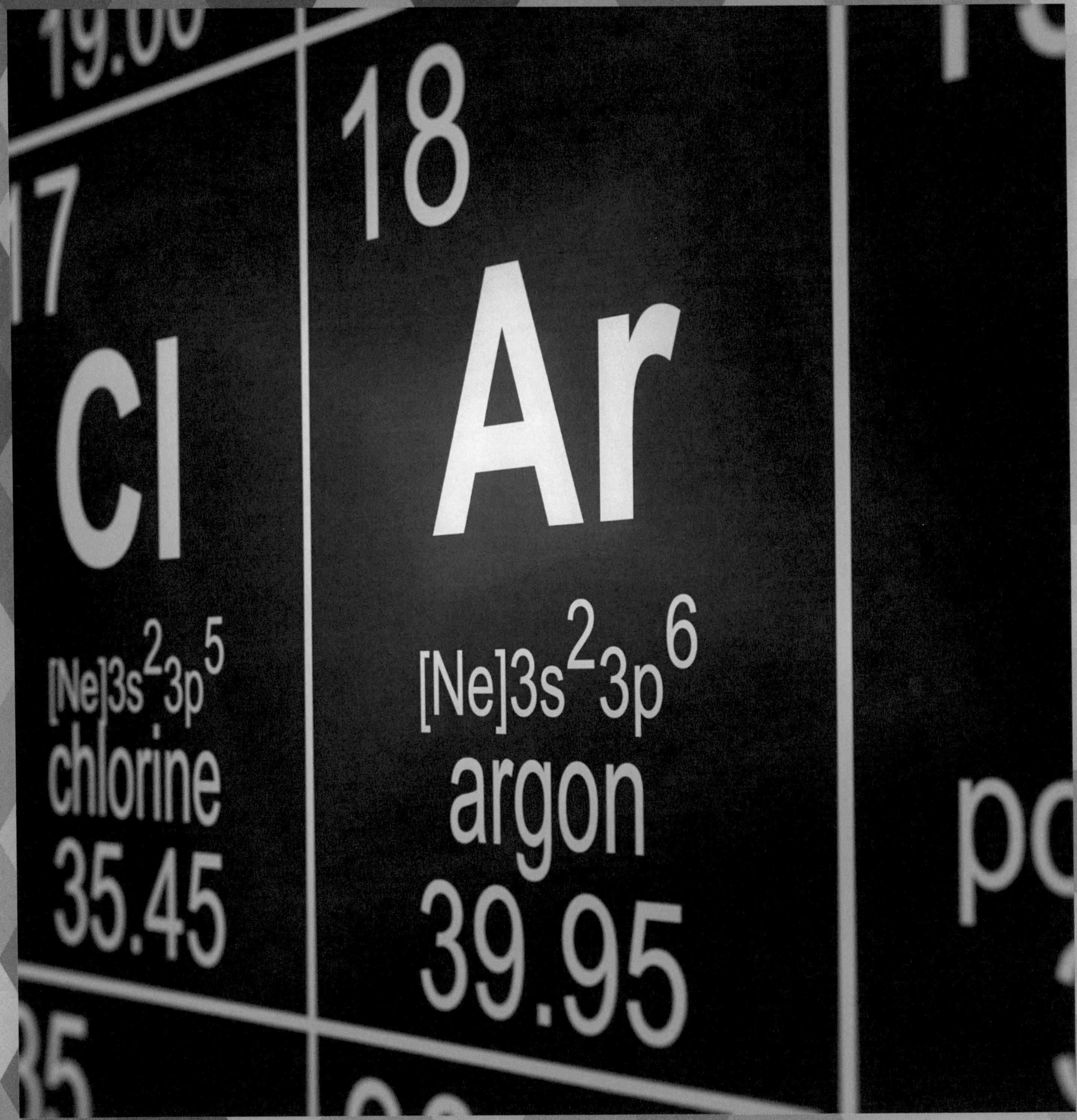

19.00

17

Cl

$[Ne]3s^2 3p^5$

chlorine

35.45

18

Ar

$[Ne]3s^2 3p^6$

argon

39.95

WHAT ARE THE NOBLE GASES?

The noble gases are located in the rightmost column of the periodic table, column 18. These elements, also called the inert gases, have a full outer shell of eight electrons except for helium, which has a full shell with only two electrons.

Because of these full shells, they very rarely combine. They are non-reactive and are also called the "inert" gases because of this characteristic. There are six noble gases. They are argon, helium, krypton, neon, radon, and xenon.

18
VIIIA
IIIA
2
4.0026
He
HELIUM
98
10
20.180

35
Br
[Ar]4s2 3d10 4p5
bromine
79.90
36
Kr
[Ar]4s2 3d10 4p6
krypton
83.80
53

WHAT PROPERTIES MAKE NOBLE GASES SIMILAR?

Since they have full outer shells, the elements of the noble gases are very stable. Because of this, they are often used in laboratory experiments where reactions need to be slowed down. Under standard conditions, they are colorless and odorless gases. They have a very narrow range where they can form liquids because their temperatures for melting and boiling are so close together.

CAN NOBLE GASES FORM BONDS?

About 40 years ago, scientists discovered that they could force the noble gases to form bonds. Some of these compounds have been used to create explosives. Under most natural conditions, the noble gases don't react with other elements.

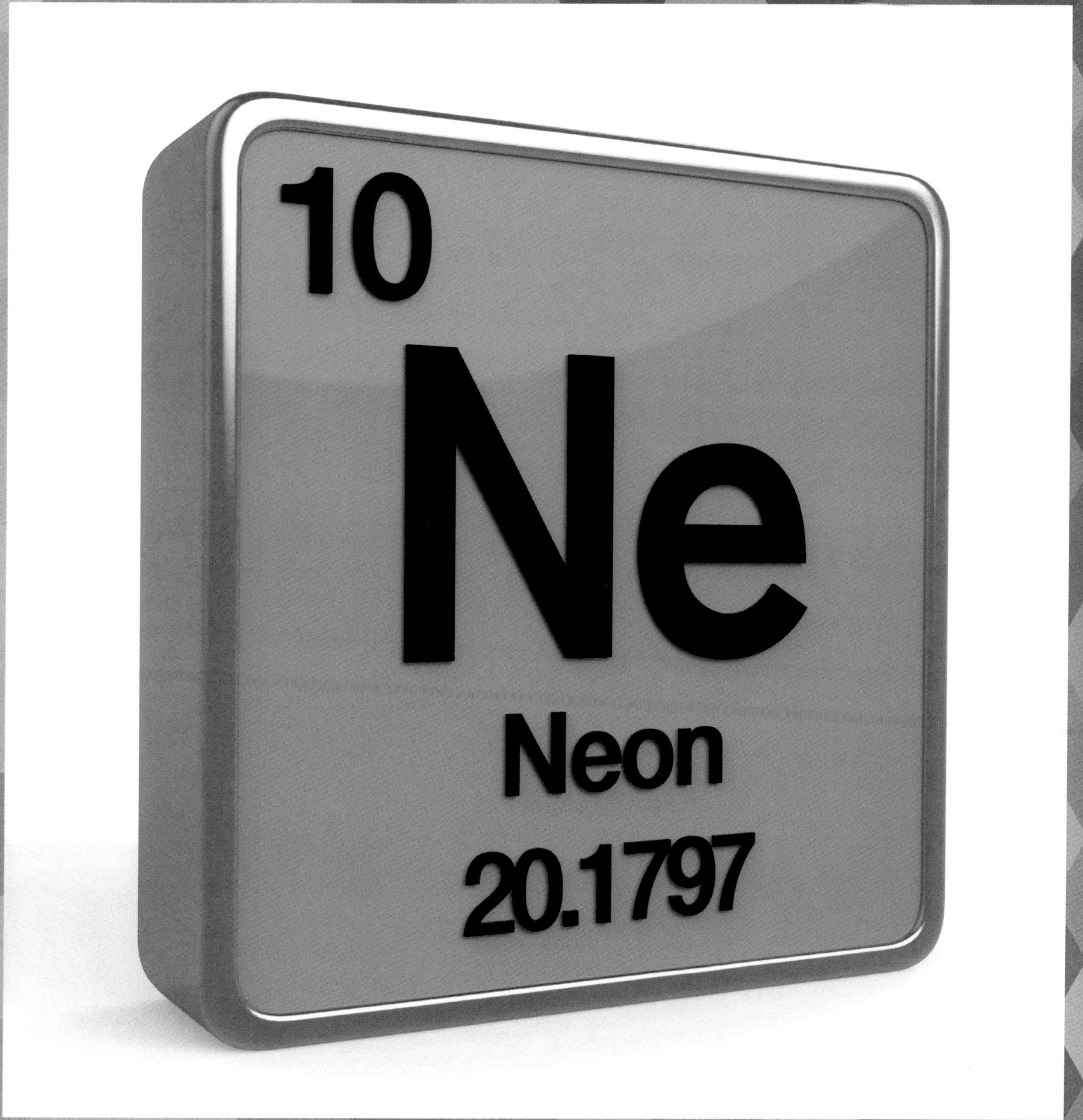

10

Ne

Neon

20.1797

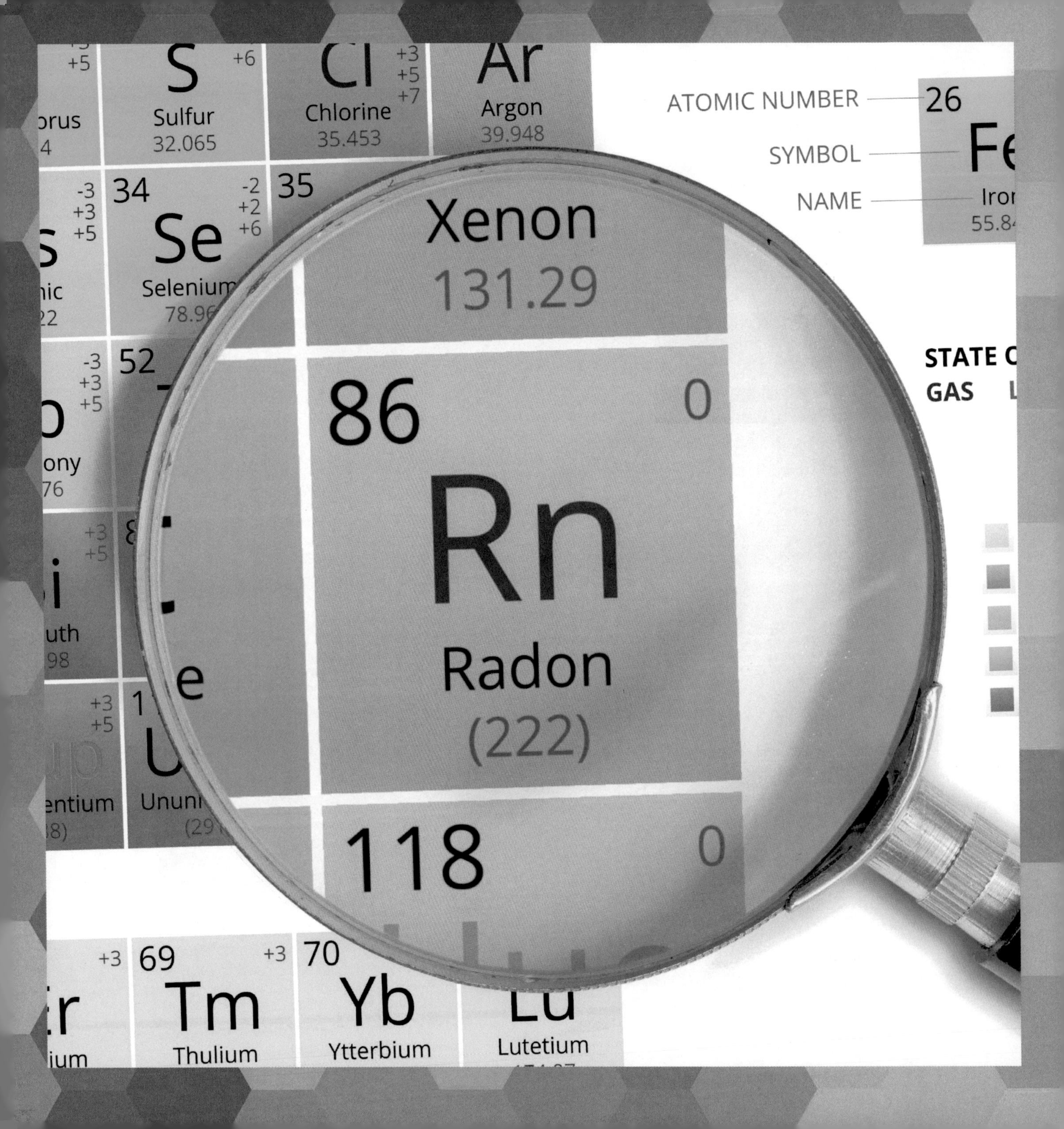

S
+6
Sulfur
32.065
Cl
+3
+5
+7
Chlorine
35.453
Ar
Argon
39.948
ATOMIC NUMBER
26
SYMBOL
NAME
34
-2
+2
+6
Se
35
Xenon
131.29
52
86
0
Rn
Radon
(222)
118
0
+3
69
Tm
Thulium
+3
70
Yb
Ytterbium
Lu
Lutetium
GAS

HOW ABUNDANT ARE THE NOBLE GASES?

On Earth, the noble gases are rare except for the element of argon, which makes up about 1% of our planet's atmosphere. It's the third most dominant gas in our atmosphere after the elements of nitrogen and oxygen.

However, throughout the universe, the abundance of the noble gases is a different story. The element of helium makes up about one-fourth of the mass of all elements in the known universe.

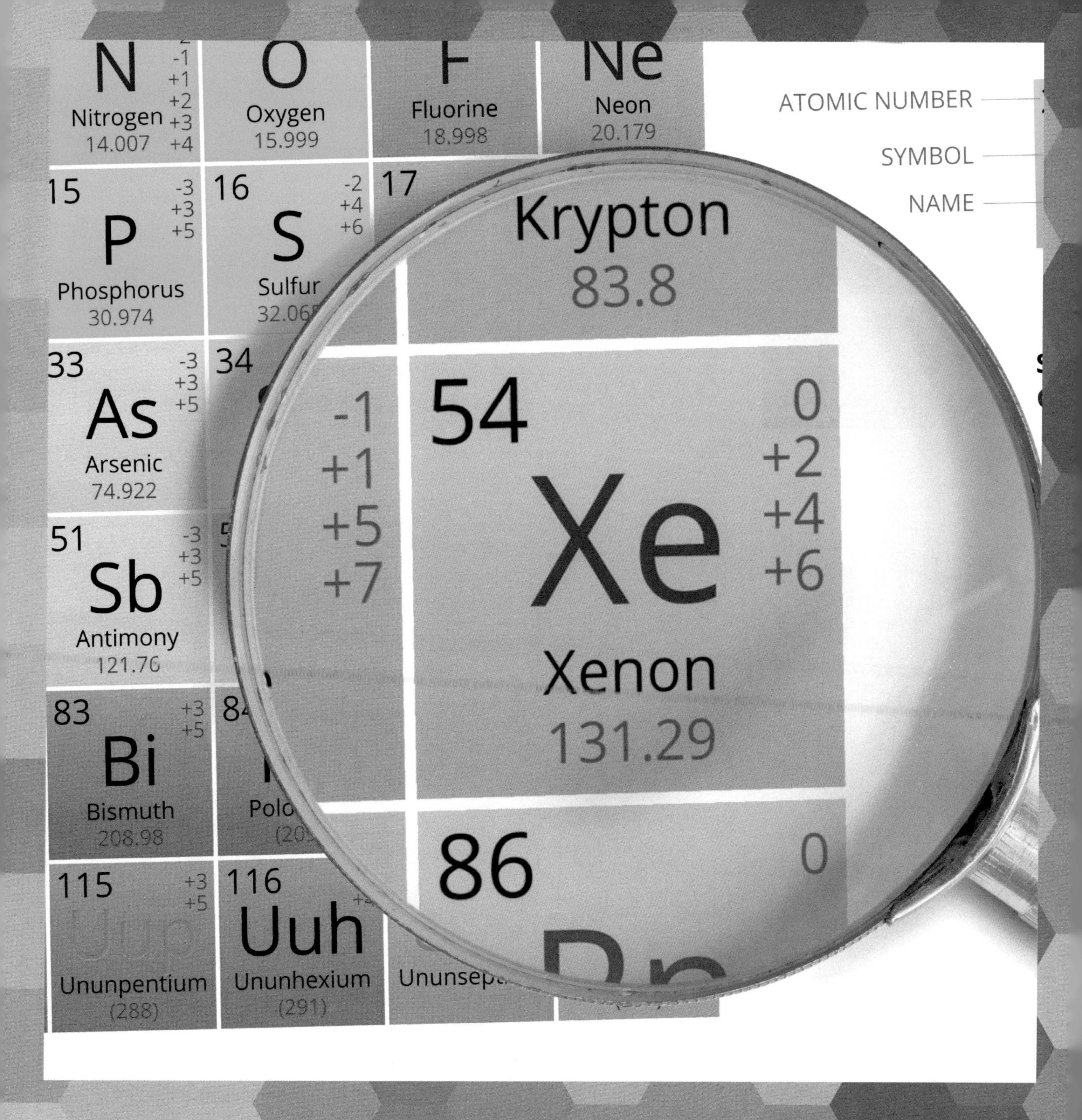
N
-1
+1
+2
+3
+4
Nitrogen
14.007
O
Oxygen
15.999
F
Fluorine
18.998
Ne
Neon
20.179
ATOMIC NUMBER
SYMBOL
NAME
15
P
-3
+3
+5
Phosphorus
30.974
16
S
-2
+4
+6
Sulfur
17
Krypton
83.8
33
As
-3
+3
+5
Arsenic
74.922
34
-1
+1
+5
+7
54
Xe
0
+2
+4
+6
Xenon
131.29
51
Sb
-3
+3
+5
Antimony
83
Bi
+3
+5
Bismuth
208.98
86
0
115
+3
+5
Uup
Ununpentium
(288)
116
Uuh
Ununhexium
(291)

INTERESTING FACTS ABOUT NOBLE, ALSO CALLED INERT, GASES

- Because it is stable and non-flammable, helium is a much safer gas to use in balloons than hydrogen is.
- The element of krypton was named after the Greek word "kryptos," which translates to "the hidden one."
- Sir William Ramsay, the Scottish chemist, discovered many of these gases.
- With the exception of radon, all the noble gases have isotopes that are stable.
- When you hear neon, you may think of neon signs, but neon signs are made of a mixture of the noble gases and other elements to achieve their bright lights in varying colors.
- The element of xenon was named after the Greek word "xenos," which means "foreigner."

WHAT ARE THE LANTHANIDES AND ACTINIDES?

The group of elements called lanthanides and the group called actinides are listed below the main part of the periodic table. There are 30 elements in both groups together and they are often called the "inner transition metals."

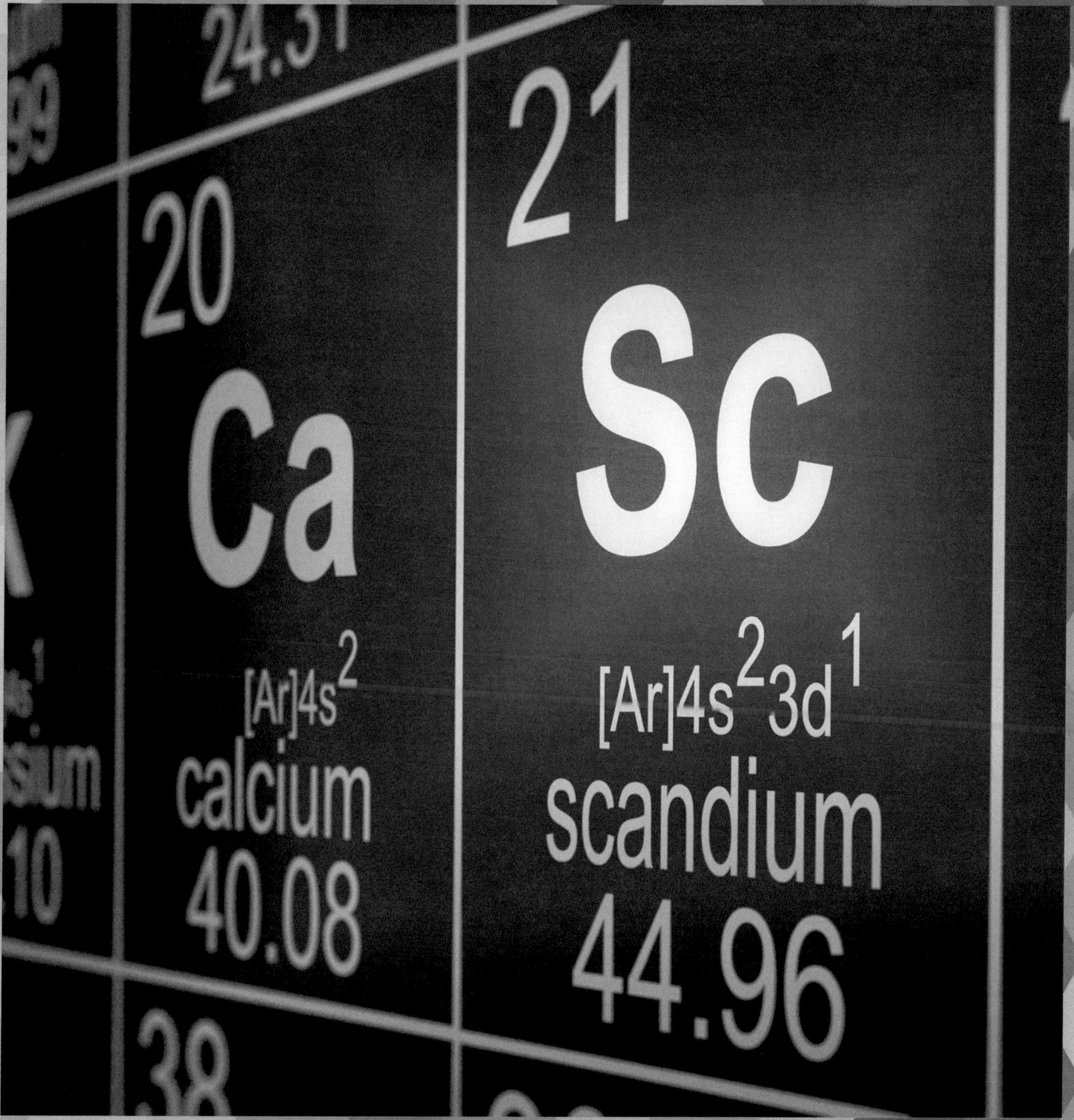

20
Ca
[Ar]4s2
calcium
40.08

21
Sc
[Ar]4s2 3d1
scandium
44.96

H
Hydrogen
1.008
2
IIA
SYMBOL
NAME
+3
Fe
Iron
55.845
3
+1
Li
Lithium
4
IIIB
LIQUID
ARTIFICIAL
11
+2
21
+3
Sc
Scandium
44.956
22
6
VIB
24
+2
+3
+6
Cr
Chromium
51.996
42
+3
+6
Mo
Molybdenum
95.94
39
+3
55
Cs
Caesium
132.91
137.33
178.49
Tantalum
180.95
+6
87
+1
Fr
88
+2
Ra
104
+4
Rf
105
+5
Db
106
Sg
Seaborgium

Their atomic numbers are in the range of 57 to 71. This group of 15 total metals is named after lanthanum since all the elements in this group have similar characteristics to this element. Along with the elements of scandium and yttrium, the lanthanides are considered to be rare.

One of the characteristics that the lanthanides share is that they are metal elements, usually silver-white in color, and they are frequently found in ores.

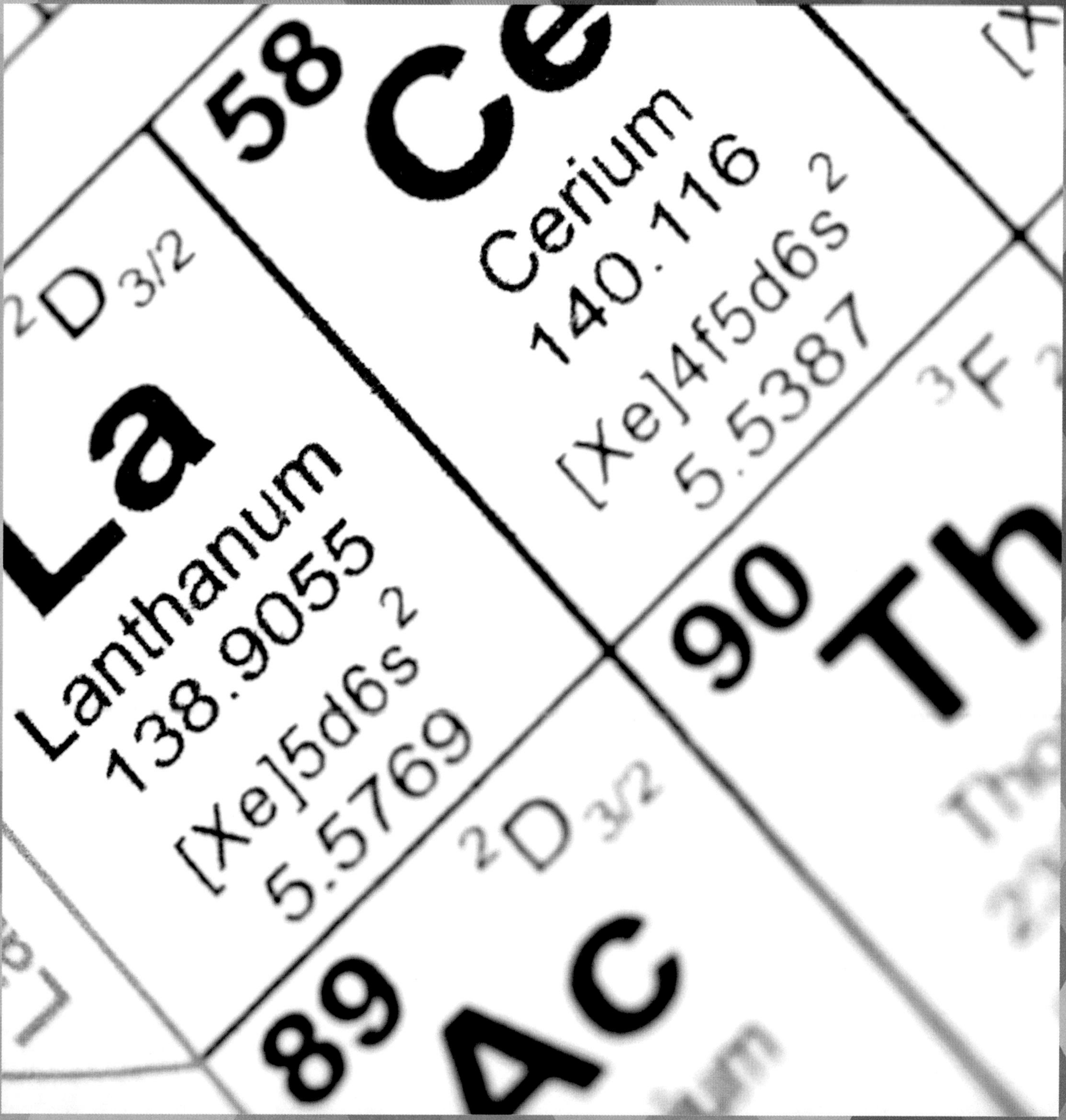

$^2D_{3/2}$
La
Lanthanum
138.9055
[Xe]5d6s^2
5.5769

58
Ce
Cerium
140.116
[Xe]4f5d6s^2
5.5387
$^3F_2$

$^2D_{3/2}$
89
Ac

90
Th

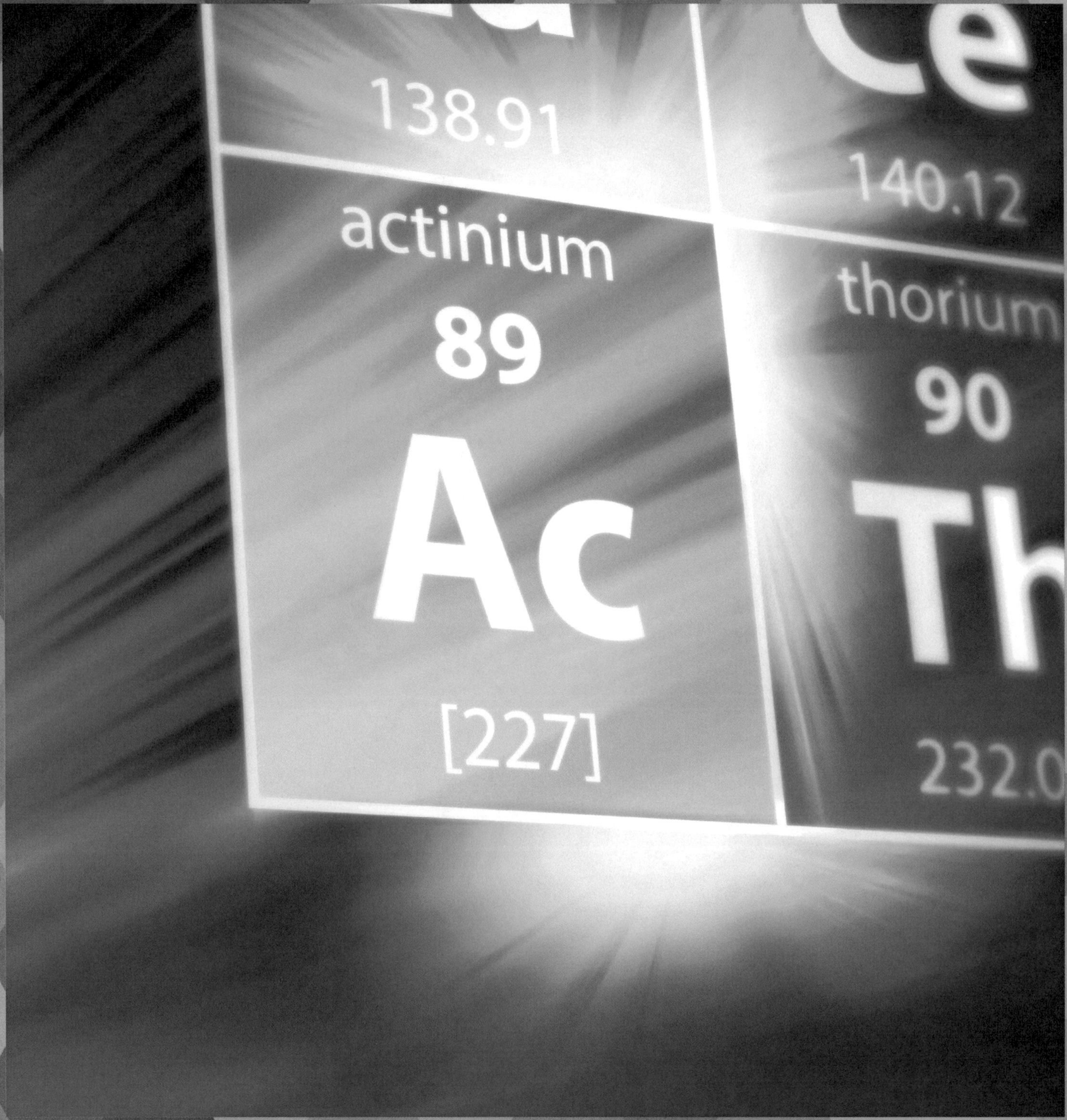

138.91
Ce
140.12
actinium
89
Ac
[227]
90

Just as the lanthanides are named after the element lanthanum, actinides are named after their first element, which is actinium. The actinide group is primarily made up of elements that are man-made, but there are a few elements that occur naturally such as thorium and uranium. There are also 15 elements in this group and their atomic numbers range from 89 to 103.

FASCINATING FACTS ABOUT LANTHANIDES AND ACTINIDES

• The elements of uranium and plutonium, which are from the actinide group, are well-known since they are used in nuclear bombs.

• Hybrid cars and magnets that are permanent as well as superconductors all use elements in the lanthanide group.

• When an element has an atomic number greater than the atomic number of 92, the number of uranium, then it is called "transuranium." Many transuranium elements are made in laboratory conditions inside nuclear reactors.

• Both groups are highly reactive when combined with halogens.

• The word "actinides" comes from the Greek word "aktis," which means ray or beam. Uranium was one of the first actinides discovered.

Periodic Table of Elements

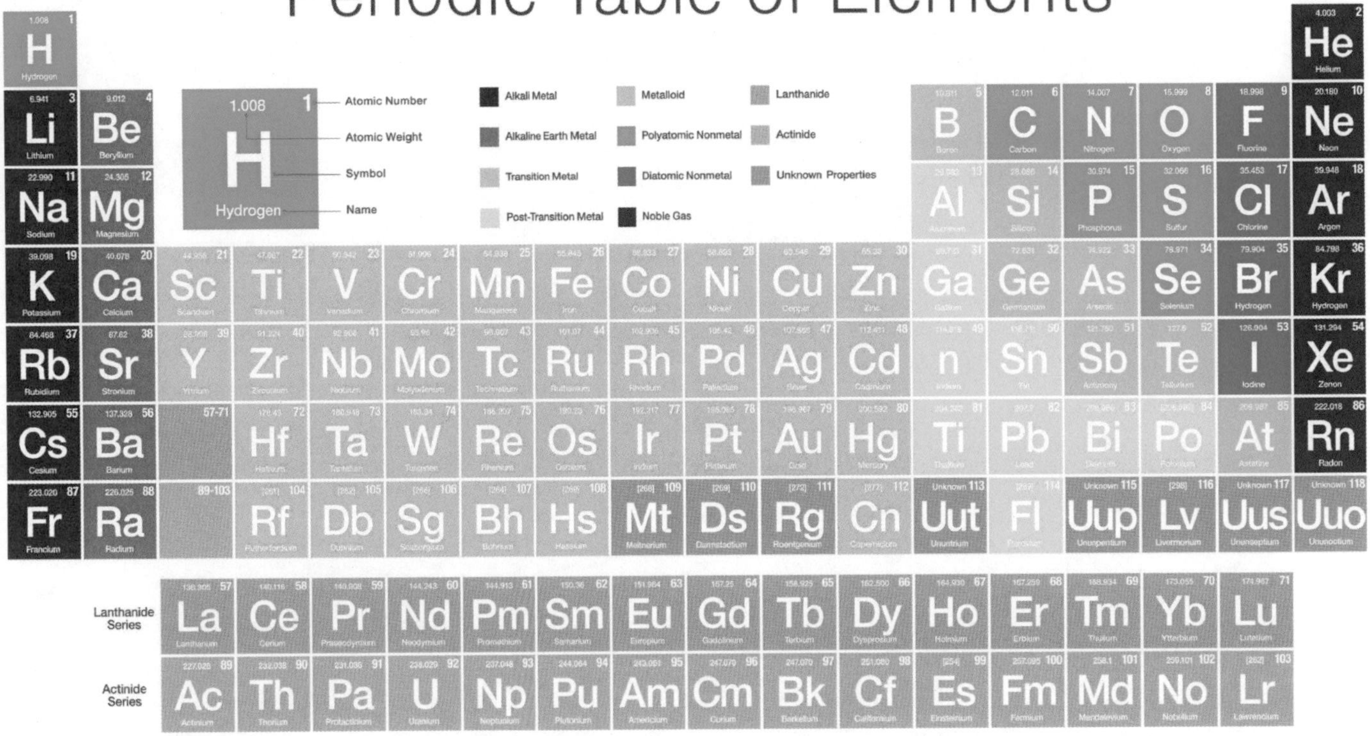

Key	
1	Atomic Number
1.008	Atomic Weight
H	Symbol
Hydrogen	Name

Alkali Metal · Alkaline Earth Metal · Transition Metal · Post-Transition Metal · Metalloid · Polyatomic Nonmetal · Diatomic Nonmetal · Noble Gas · Lanthanide · Actinide · Unknown Properties

1	2	3	4	5	6	7	8	9	10	11	12	13	14	15	16	17	18
1.008 1 H Hydrogen																	4.003 2 He Helium
6.941 3 Li Lithium	9.012 4 Be Beryllium											10.811 5 B Boron	12.011 6 C Carbon	14.007 7 N Nitrogen	15.999 8 O Oxygen	18.998 9 F Fluorine	20.180 10 Ne Neon
22.990 11 Na Sodium	24.305 12 Mg Magnesium											26.982 13 Al Aluminum	28.086 14 Si Silicon	30.974 15 P Phosphorus	32.066 16 S Sulfur	35.453 17 Cl Chlorine	39.948 18 Ar Argon
39.098 19 K Potassium	40.078 20 Ca Calcium	44.956 21 Sc Scandium	47.867 22 Ti Titanium	50.942 23 V Vanadium	51.996 24 Cr Chromium	54.938 25 Mn Manganese	55.845 26 Fe Iron	58.933 27 Co Cobalt	58.693 28 Ni Nickel	63.546 29 Cu Copper	65.38 30 Zn Zinc	69.723 31 Ga Gallium	72.631 32 Ge Germanium	74.922 33 As Arsenic	78.971 34 Se Selenium	79.904 35 Br Hydrogen	84.798 36 Kr Hydrogen
84.468 37 Rb Rubidium	87.62 38 Sr Stronium	88.906 39 Y Yttrium	91.224 40 Zr Zirconium	92.906 41 Nb Niobium	95.96 42 Mo Molybdenum	98.907 43 Tc Technetium	101.07 44 Ru Ruthenium	102.906 45 Rh Rhodium	106.42 46 Pd Palladium	107.868 47 Ag Silver	112.411 48 Cd Cadmium	114.818 49 n Indium	118.71 50 Sn Tin	121.760 51 Sb Antimony	127.6 52 Te Tellurium	126.904 53 I Iodine	131.294 54 Xe Zenon
132.905 55 Cs Cesium	137.328 56 Ba Barium	57-71	178.49 72 Hf Hafnium	180.948 73 Ta Tantalum	183.84 74 W Tungsten	186.207 75 Re Rhenium	190.23 76 Os Osmium	192.217 77 Ir Iridium	195.085 78 Pt Platinum	196.967 79 Au Gold	200.592 80 Hg Mercury	204.383 81 Ti Thallium	207.2 82 Pb Lead	208.980 83 Bi Bismuth	[208.982] 84 Po Polonium	209.987 85 At Astatine	222.018 86 Rn Radon
223.020 87 Fr Francium	226.025 88 Ra Radium	89-103	[261] 104 Rf Rutherfordium	[262] 105 Db Dubnium	[266] 106 Sg Seaborgium	[264] 107 Bh Bohrium	[269] 108 Hs Hassium	[268] 109 Mt Meitnerium	[269] 110 Ds Darmstadtium	[272] 111 Rg Roentgenium	[277] 112 Cn Copernicium	Unknown 113 Uut Ununtrium	[289] 114 Fl Flerovium	Unknown 115 Uup Ununpentium	[298] 116 Lv Livermorium	Unknown 117 Uus Ununseptium	Unknown 118 Uuo Ununoctium

Series															
Lanthanide Series	138.905 57 La Lanthanum	140.116 58 Ce Cerium	140.908 59 Pr Praseodymium	144.243 60 Nd Neodymium	144.913 61 Pm Promethium	150.36 62 Sm Samarium	151.964 63 Eu Europium	157.25 64 Gd Gadolinium	158.925 65 Tb Terbium	162.500 66 Dy Dysprosium	164.930 67 Ho Holmium	167.259 68 Er Erbium	168.934 69 Tm Thulium	173.055 70 Yb Ytterbium	174.967 71 Lu Lutetium
Actinide Series	227.028 89 Ac Actinium	232.038 90 Th Thorium	231.036 91 Pa Protactinium	238.029 92 U Uranium	237.048 93 Np Neptunium	244.064 94 Pu Plutonium	243.061 95 Am Americium	247.070 96 Cm Curium	247.070 97 Bk Berkelium	251.080 98 Cf Californium	[254] 99 Es Einsteinium	257.095 100 Fm Fermium	258.1 101 Md Mendelevium	259.101 102 No Nobelium	[262] 103 Lr Lawrencium

Awesome! Now that you've read this book you know more about Chemistry and the Periodic Table including the halogens and the noble gases. You also learned about the lanthanides and actinides. You can find more Chemistry books from Baby Professor by searching the website of your favorite book retailer.

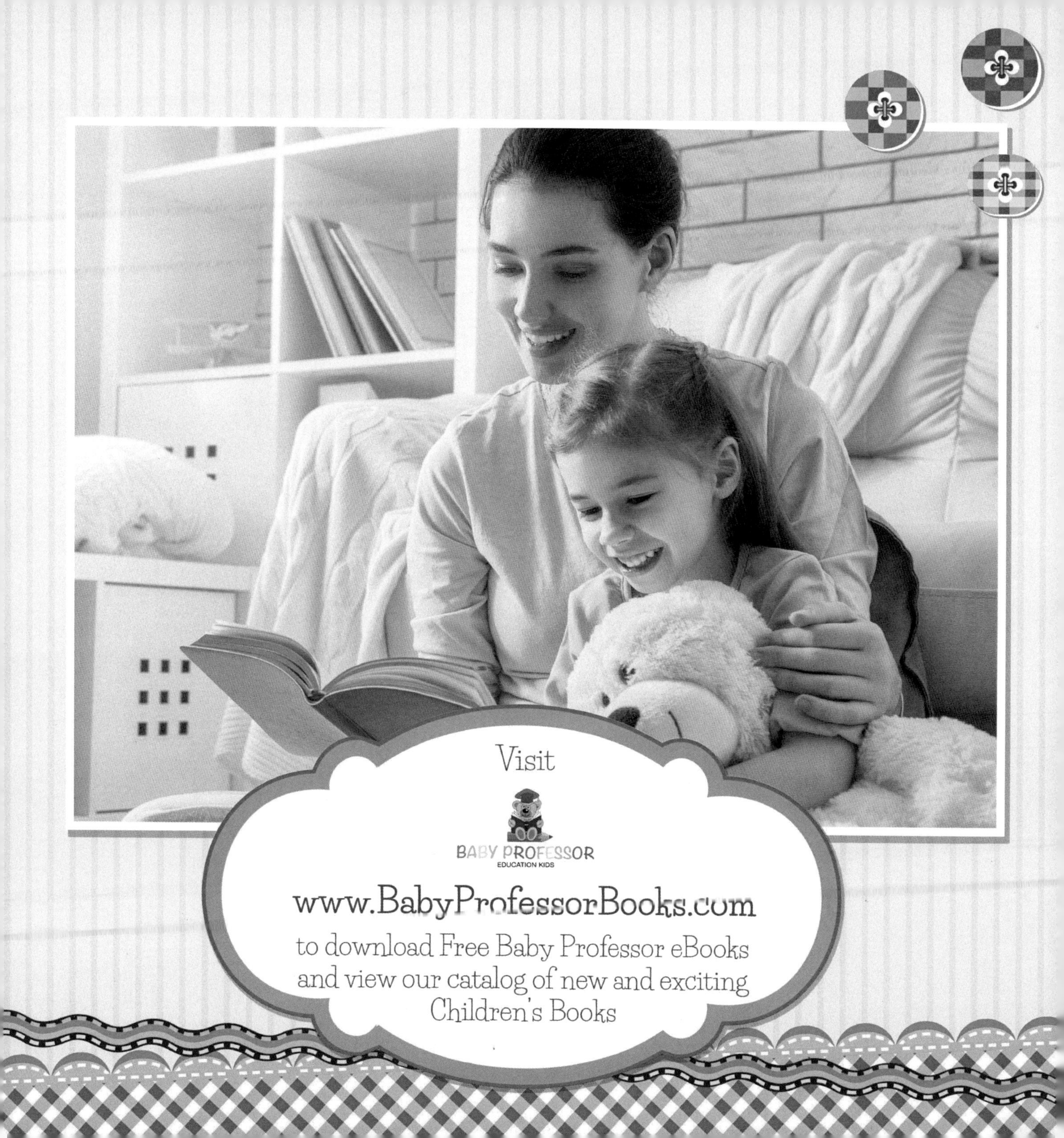

Visit
BABY PROFESSOR
EDUCATION KIDS
www.BabyProfessorBooks.com
to download Free Baby Professor eBooks and view our catalog of new and exciting Children's Books

Made in the USA
Las Vegas, NV
28 November 2023